Animal Soup

Emily Manuel Reeves, LPC

Illustrated by
S. Murray Gayheart

EM Books

Savannah, Georgia

To the Reader

Just like a homemade soup, these characters (mostly animal) mix the right ingredients to help elementary-aged children (and the young of heart) feel much better when facing life challenges. This collection of animal characters forms a kind of nourishing Animal Soup. At the end of each small story, the reader will find a helpful hint to help children make good choices in life.

I developed these stories while providing counseling services to elementary school children who were living in a foster care setting. These children provided me with much inspiration to write this book.

My hope is that you will enjoy *Animal Soup* and have a life that is full of enjoyment and reading!

Emily Manuel Reeves, LPC

ISBN 978-0-9821506-0-3
Copyright © 2009 by Emily Manuel Reeves

To my daughter Caroline, for your patience as I have worked on this project, and to my family and friends for your encouragement

Table of Contents

The Bothersome Bubble (about friendship) / 6

Grover the Groundhog (about courage) / 14

The Impatient Squirrel (about patience) / 20

Jack in the Box (about resiliency) / 26

Patches (about sharing) / 32

The Red Kettle (about self-care) / 42

Shiloh (about self-confidence) / 48

Sour Grapes (about compromise) / 56

Stone Faced Susan (about feelings) / 62

The Bothersome Bubble

It is lots of fun to blow bubbles! But it is even more fun to be one.

Hi! My name is Bobby the Bubble. I would like to share with you about what it is like to be a bubble. Bubbles get to fly high in the sky and float through the air. Wow! It is beautiful up there in the great, blue sky! It is really neat to look down at all the people on the ground. They look so very small when you are high up in the sky. We enjoy looking down at the people and they enjoy looking up at us too!

As you probably know, bubbles come in all shapes and sizes just like people. We have different personalities, too. Some bubbles enjoy sticking together with other bubbles. Other bubbles just like to be left alone. I am sure you know people like this, too. Other bubbles are in a hurry and glide through the air quickly. I bet sometimes you are in a hurry, too.

I am happy to say that I get along with most bubbles. However, one day I met this bubble that I call the Bothersome Bubble. He would glide next to another bubble and just pop him for no reason at all. We did not like this. I imagine if you were a bubble you would not like to be popped either! My bubble friends and I decided that we would not play with this bubble any more.

*Helpful Hint: Bobby the Bubble hopes that you do not act mean to others. If you do, he hopes that you will stop picking on other people so that you can keep your friends.

C.A.L.M. is The Way Bobby the Bubble Solves Problems

1. C—COOL OFF. You can count to ten, take a deep breath, Imagine yourself blowing bubbles, etc.. in order for you to calm down when mad.
2. A—Agree to get help (from an adult) or come up with a plan to solve the problem (example: ignoring, flipping a coin, taking turns.)
3. L—Listen to the person you are having the problem with. Look at them when they are talking. Stop what you are doing and listen. Then, take turns speaking until you and the other person can repeat what the other is saying or feeling.
4. M—Make Good Choices in order to keep good friendships.

Grover the Ground Hog

If you do not know already, groundhogs spend most of their time living under the ground. Grover has been dreading February the 2nd. This day has been named Groundhog Day. On this day, humans try their best to predict an early or late spring. "They need the help from the groundhogs, of course!" exclaims Grover.

Grover has never been above ground. "I have heard stories from older groundhogs" said Grover. They tell Grover, "It will be fun to be the one to predict the weather for the humans." Grover trembles at the thought. "I have never seen my own shadow. I do not know what it is like to be above ground."

The days seem to speed by for Grover. It is finally February 2nd, Groundhog Day. "I am not ready!" says Grover. "You have to be," says the ground hog who helped predict last year's late Spring.

"Here everyone comes," says Grover. Hours pass. Finally, a man with a deep voice announces, "Grover predicts that we will have an early Spring!" Grover was excited about what he saw. "It was actually not scary after all. There were lots of smiling faces. Above ground was very pretty with all the trees and pretty flowers."

Grover was not scared any more. His shadow was only his shadow. And being above ground was not like he had feared.

*Helpful Hint: Grover wants you to trust in yourself. We all get scared sometimes, but that is normal. It helps to talk to others and get help when we need it to stay safe.

The Impatient Squirrel

Sammy the Squirrel lived with his wife and his newborn baby squirrel in Pecan Hollow. He was beginning to prepare for the Winter. Since he was a young squirrel, he had been told to wait until Autumn for the pecans to fall from the trees. "Well," Sammy thought, "I do not want to wait until Autumn. I want to have more food stored than any squirrel in Pecan Hollow.

So when Summer approached, Sammy went to the forest and began to shake the trees. No pecans fell! Sammy became frustrated. "I want the food now," said Sammy. He had another idea. "I will water the trees and maybe the pecans will be ready to eat earlier." This did not work either. By this time, Sammy had given up. He was exhausted.

Autumn was finally here. Everyone else was working and storing nuts for the winter. Sammy did not have any pecans. He noticed that the other squirrels had enough to keep them through the winter. They were nice enough to share some extra food with Sammy and his family.

Sammy told himself, "Next year I will wait until Autumn to look for my food." Sammy learned that being patient helps after all.

*Helpful Hint: Sammy hopes that you are patient but if you are not, he hopes that you will learn how to wait. Sammy found out there are some things that can not be hurried no matter what you try to do.

Jack in the Box

There once lived a boy named Jack. His home was a small red box. Everyone in the neighborhood knew Jack. Jack was like a clown. Oh, how fun he was to be around! He was always laughing and telling jokes.

One day, Jack learned some sad news. From that day on, Jack did not come out of his red box any more. Days passed and no one saw Jack. People became concerned. They tried to shake the box.

Nothing happened . . . . They also tried to talk very loud into the box, but Jack did not answer. Finally, Fred, a little boy who always came to visit Jack, had an idea. Fred said, "I am going to turn the knob on Jack's red box."

Guess what? Out popped Jack! Fred's eyes gleamed with excitement as he looked at Jack. Jack began to giggle. He was so happy that people missed hearing his jokes.

*Helpful Hint: Jack says that even though you might feel stuck, you can always pop back up. It might take some help from someone else— someone like a friend—but you can get better and feel better!

Patches

Everybody thought Lucy's new puppy was so cute. "What are you going to call him?" Lucy was asked. "I like the name Patches," said Lucy. "He has black ears, a black tail, and patches of white all over his body." Everyone agreed that Patches was the best name for this puppy.

Lucy's friend got a new puppy a few months later. They decided to let Patches play with Frisky, the new puppy. They had lots of Patches' toys to play with: a worn out tennis ball, a big white bone, yesterday's newspaper, and a bright orange squeaky toy. Frisky thought, "Oh, how much fun this will be to meet a new friend and play with all these toys!"

After Patches met Frisky, he gathered up all his toys and hid the toys very carefully so Frisky could not find them. First, he hid the tennis ball under the sofa. Next, he buried the big, white bone in the yard. Then he hid the newspaper in the bushes. And the bright orange squeaky toy was hidden in Lucy's sandbox. Patches did not want to share his toys with Frisky. Frisky decided to go home. He knew that he would have more fun running in his own yard than being at Patches' house. "It is no fun to play with someone who does not share," thought Frisky.

The next day Patches went to look for all his toys. He looked all over and could not find the tennis ball, the big white bone, yesterday's newspaper, or even the bright orange, squeaky toy. Patches forgot where he put the toys. He hid them from himself!

Patches thought, "I got what I deserved." The next day he went by Frisky's house to apologize for not sharing his toys.

*Helpful Hint: Patches says, "If you do not share your toys, you cannot expect others to share with you, either. Remember, treat people kindly."

The Red Kettle

Sandy rarely drank hot tea. Her red kettle had never been used. It was kept on the second shelf in the kitchen pantry. The kettle was comfortable there and knew what was expected of it.

One day, Sandy had friends over. She needed to boil water in the kettle. The kettle was taken off its comfortable shelf. It was then placed on the stove and water was poured inside. Let me make it clear. The purpose of a kettle is to boil water. However, this red kettle had never been used before. It did not know what to do. On the outside, it looked like any other kettle. It was practically new. The color was bright red, and it had a black handle. On the inside, it felt out of control and did not know how to react to the boiling water inside.

After the water had boiled, Sandy took the kettle and poured the water in the tea cups. She then added the tea bags and sugar for her friends to enjoy at the tea party.

The kettle began to feel much better. It was no longer holding the boiling water inside. The red kettle thought, "Next time, I will be better prepared to boil water, and I will not feel out of control." After Sandy's friends left, she took the red kettle back to its home, the pantry. "It is nice to be back in my safe place for a while," thought the red kettle.

*Helpful Hint: The red kettle says, "Sometimes we cannot be in control of everything in our lives. That is OK. It is important to take care of yourself in the meantime. It is also important to have a safe place where you can go to relax and have time for yourself."

Shiloh

Once upon a time there was a dog named Shiloh. Shiloh lived with his owner. Shiloh would often hunt with his owner. When he was not hunting, he would run and play with his best dog friend, Alex.

Every where Shiloh went, he would carry his favorite white bone. He would take it hunting. He would take it when he played with Alex. He would take it to the store and even when he went to bed at night.

One day Alex asked to borrow his bone. "NO! exclaimed Shiloh. Shiloh could not imagine what he would do without his bone.

The very next day, Shiloh lost his bone. He could not find it anywhere. "Oh, no!, shouted Shiloh.

He looked everywhere but he could not find the bone. His owner asked, "Would you go to the store with me to get your favorite dog food?" Shiloh wanted to go but said, "I can't because I do not have my bone." His owner told him that he could not get his favorite dog food unless he came along. Shiloh decided to go.

Guess what? Shiloh discovered, "I can go places without my old white bone. It was actually more fun without the bone because I have both of my paws free when I go hunting now. I don't have to worry about dropping my bone! When I go to the store, I can carry more things with me. Most importantly, when I am playing with my best dog friend, I often win our running races now because my bone would often fall out of my mouth!"

Shiloh was surprised that he did not need the bone any more! He felt happy inside and he looked happy on the outside too!

*Helpful Hint: Shiloh wants you to know that if you believe in yourself, you can accomplish a whole lot! So do not hold yourself back like Shiloh did when he took the old, white bone with him everywhere! It just got in his way.

Sour Grapes

Out in the vineyard lived a bunch of grapes. These grapes were actually a family which consisted of the papa grape, the mama grape and the children grapes. The whole bunch was grown on the same soil. They received the same amount of shade, sunlight, and water. All were sweet on the inside except for one of the young grapes. Her name was Ginny. On the outside, Ginny looked like all the other grapes, but in the inside she was all sour.

Ginny did not like to mix with the other grapes. When she did mix with them, they had to do whatever Ginny wanted to do or else she would throw a temper tantrum and act all sour. One day, a lady was walking through the vineyard and was about to pick the whole bunch of grapes (Ginny and her family).

Then the lady noticed that one of the grapes (Ginny) was all sour on the inside. The lady took almost all of the grapes with her EXCEPT for Ginny.

Ginny became frightened. She realized that she really wanted to hang out with the rest of the bunch of grapes after all.

From that day on, Ginny decided to stop acting all sour. Instead, she let the sweetness that was already there come out.

*Helpful Hint: Ginny wants you to know that you can still have fun even if you do not get your way all the time!

Stone-Faced Susan

Once upon a time, there was a little girl named Susan. She enjoyed playing with her sister and especially playing jump rope.

One day this all changed. Her family started to have problems. Susan was upset and did not know what to do. To protect herself, she stopped speaking. When Susan would have a bad day or when something would not go her way, she would put on a stone face. When her friends and family looked at her face, all they saw was a stone statue.

Susan's friends were sad and did not know how to help her. One day they had a meeting. Molly, Susan's sister and Sara, her friend, decided: "Let's go get a bucket of water and pour it over her head. Maybe that will wash the stone away!" So that is what they did. They went and filled up a old yellow bucket with water. They had to carry the bucket together because it was so heavy. Next, they poured it over Susan's head.

All of a sudden, Susan's face was alive and cheerful again! They screamed with delight! The children had washed the stone face away.

Wow, Susan was amazed. "People really care for me… A stone face does not help me. Instead, it keeps me from being happy. From now on, I will go outside and play with my friends or talk to someone when I have a bad day."

*Helpful Hint: Susan hopes that you will not put on a stone face when you have a bad day or a problem. She hopes that you will talk to someone or play with your friends like she has decided to do.

EMILY REEVES is native of Savannah, Georgia. She is a Licensed Professional Counselor who works as a guidance counselor in the public schools. She has taught at the college level and conducts many seminars in her field. Married with one daughter, Emily enjoys spending time with her family, going to the beach, swimming, and running. She can be reached at www.storiesbyemily.com

www.ingramcontent.com/pod-product-compliance
Lightning Source LLC
LaVergne TN
LVHW071650060526
838200LV00029B/419